Little Q™

Getting to Know
Animals

A Little Q™ Electronic Workbook

Illustrated by Kelly McMahon

PRICE STERN SLOAN

Los Angeles

The Fun Way to Start Learning

This book is specially designed for use with the **Little Q Electronic Answer Wand.** When the Little Q answer wand is moved over the pages of a **Little Q Electronic Workbook** it detects correct and incorrect answers and responds with "right" or "wrong" sounds and lights.

The Little Q Electronic Learning System has been created to equip the 3 to 6-year-old with the all-important basic skills, and is simple enough for children to use all by themselves. The bright, easy-to-handle Little Q wand plus the colorful, interactive **Little Q Electronic Library** of books provide a structured learning environment for children as they begin to understand reading and mathematics.

Little Q has reinvented the 3 Rs to help children learn in the most efficient way.

Recognition   Children recognize concepts by associating pictures, words and numbers.

Repetition   Activities are designed to be done again and again, reinforcing ideas and helping children remember what they learn.

Reward   The "beeping " and "buzzing" sounds and flashing lights make little children feel terrific.

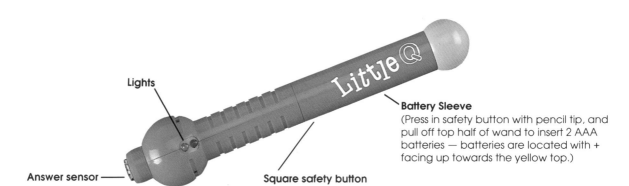

Lights

Battery Sleeve
(Press in safety button with pencil tip, and pull off top half of wand to insert 2 AAA batteries — batteries are located with + facing up towards the yellow top.)

Answer sensor

Square safety button

Concept Roger Burrows *M. Ed.,* **Educational Consultants** Deborah Christine *M. Ed.* & Stevie Mack *M. Ed.*
Book Development, Design and Production Morgan-Slade & Associates, Menlo Park, CA

Try Little Q here
You can **press** or **track** answers with Little Q!

PRESS
Press Little Q firmly on the rectangle and triangle below

Green light
and "beep"

Red light
and "buzz"

TRACK
Keep Little Q pressed on the page as you track through the answers

Start
Tracking

Stop
tracking

Little Q's batteries need replacing when it reads all answers as correct

birds

birds

fish

fish

cats

cats

rabbits

rabbits

dogs

dogs

sheep

sheep

horses

horses

beavers

beavers

COWS

COWS

elephants

elephants

turtles